☆ TRUMPET ☆ STARS ☆

SET 2

BY H.A. VANDERCOOK

A COLLECTION OF TRUMPET SOLOS WITH PIANO ACCOMPANIMENT

T0045664

CONTENTS

ISBN 978-0-634-03590-6

RUBANK®

HAL•LEONARD®
CORPORATION
7777 W. BLUEMOUND RD. P.O. BOX 13819 MILWAUKEE, WI 53213

Visit Hal Leonard Online at
www.halleonard.com

Written by H.A Vandercook, *Trumpet Stars, Sets 1 & 2,* have combined some of Rubank's most popular solos into two collections. After years of remaining the favorite trumpet repertoire pieces of students and teachers, these new book/CD packages provide a unique approach to a better understanding and enjoyment of the music. Tracks 1-6 offers a full performance for trumpet and piano, while Tracks 7-12 has piano accompaniment only. Whether for practice or for listening enjoyment, these book/CD editions will be superb additions to any trumpet music collection.

SPICA

Progressive Etudes for Cornet or Trumpet

Copyright MCMXXXVIII by Rubank Inc., Chicago, Ill.
International Copyright Secured

Spica

7

Spica

CENTAURUS
Progressive Etudes for Cornet or Trumpet

Centaurus

Faster

TRIO

TRIO

Centaurus

Centaurus

ORION

Progressive Etudes for Cornet or Trumpet

Copyright MCMXXXVIII by Rubank Inc. Chicago, Ill.
International Copyright Secured

Orion

14

Orion

TRUMPET ☆ STARS

SET 2

BY H.A. VANDERCOOK

A COLLECTION OF TRUMPET SOLOS WITH PIANO ACCOMPANIMENT

CONTENTS

ISBN 978-0-634-03590-6

RUBANK®

HAL•LEONARD®
CORPORATION
7777 W. BLUEMOUND RD. P.O. BOX 13819 MILWAUKEE, WI 53213

Visit Hal Leonard Online at
www.halleonard.com

Written by H.A Vandercook, *Trumpet Stars, Sets 1 & 2,* have combined some of Rubank's most popular solos into two collections. After years of remaining the favorite trumpet repertoire pieces of students and teachers, these new book/CD packages provide a unique approach to a better understanding and enjoyment of the music. Tracks 1-6 offers a full performance for trumpet and piano, while Tracks 7-12 has piano accompaniment only. Whether for practice or for listening enjoyment, these book/CD editions will be superb additions to any trumpet music collection.

SPICA

Progressive Etudes for Cornet or Trumpet

Copyright MCMXXXVIII by Rubank Inc., Chicago, Ill.
International Copyright Secured

CENTAURUS
Progressive Etudes for Cornet or Trumpet

Copyright MCMXXXVIII by Rubank Inc. Chicago, Ill.
International Copyright Secured

ORION

Progressive Etudes for Cornet or Trumpet

Copyright MCMXXXVIII by Rubank Inc. Chicago, Ill.
International Copyright Secured

SIRIUS

Progressive Etudes for Cornet or Trumpet

MIRA
Progressive Etudes for Cornet or Trumpet

Mira

RIGEL
Progressive Etudes for Cornet or Trumpet

Copyright MCMXXXVIII by Rubank Inc., Chicago, Ill.
International Copyright Secured

Orion

SIRIUS

Progressive Etudes for Cornet or Trumpet

Copyright MCMXXXVIII by Rubank Inc. Chicago, Ill.
International Copyright Secured

MIRA

Progressive Etudes for Cornet or Trumpet

Copyright MCMXXXVIII by Rubank Inc. Chicago, Ill.
International Copyright Secured

21

Mira

Mira

23

Mira

RIGEL
Progressive Etudes for Cornet or Trumpet

Copyright MCMXXXVIII by Rubank Inc., Chicago, Ill.
International Copyright Secured

Rigal

TRIO *bold*

Rigal

Rigal